Using Mac OS X
Mavericks

Kevin Wilson

Apress®

Using Mac OS X Mavericks

ISBN-13 (pbk): 978-1-4302-6682-2

ISBN-13 (electronic): 978-1-4302-6683-9

President and Publisher: Paul Manning

Lead Editor: Steve Anglin

Developmental Editor: James Markham

Editorial Board: Steve Anglin, Mark Beckner, Ewan Buckingham, Gary Cornell, Louise Corrigan, Jim DeWolf, Jonathan Gennick, Jonathan Hassell, Robert Hutchinson, Michelle Lowman, James Markham, Matthew Moodie, Jeff Olson, Jeffrey Pepper, Douglas Pundick, Ben Renow-Clarke, Dominic Shakeshaft, Gwenan Spearing, Matt Wade, Steve Weiss

Coordinating Editor: Jill Balzano

Copy Editor: April Rondeau

Compositor: SPi Global

Indexer: SPi Global

Artist: SPi Global

Cover Designer: Anna Ishchenko

Distributed to the book trade worldwide by Springer Science+Business Media New York, 233 Spring Street, 6th Floor, New York, NY 10013. Phone 1-800-SPRINGER, fax (201) 348-4505, email orders-ny@springer-sbm.com, or visit www.springeronline.com. Apress Media, LLC is a California LLC and the sole member (owner) is Springer Science + Business Media Finance Inc (SSBM Finance Inc). SSBM Finance Inc is a Delaware corporation.

For information on translations, please email rights@apress.com, or visit www.apress.com.

Apress and friends of ED books may be purchased in bulk for academic, corporate, or promotional use. eBook versions and licenses are also available for most titles. For more information, reference our Special Bulk Sales–eBook Licensing web page at www.apress.com/bulk-sales.

Contents at a Glance

About the Author

Kevin Wilson, a practicing computer engineer and tutor, has had a passion for gadgets, cameras, computers, and technology for many years.

After graduating with a Masters in computer science, software engineering & multimedia systems, he has worked in the computer industry supporting and working with many different types of computer systems, and also worked in education running specialist lessons on film making and visual effects for young people. He has also worked as an IT tutor, has taught in colleges in South Africa, and has been a tutor for adult education in England.

His books were written in the hope that they will help people to use their computer with greater understanding, productivity, and efficiency—to help students and people in countries like South Africa who have never used a computer before. It is his hope that they will get the same benefits from computer technology as we do.

Acknowledgments

Thanks to all the staff at Apress for their passion, dedication, and hard work in the preparation and production of this book.

To all my friends and family for their continued support and encouragement in all my writing projects.

To all my colleagues, students, and testers who took the time to test procedures and offer feedback on the book.

Finally, thanks to you, the reader, for choosing this book. I hope it helps you use your computer with greater ease. .

Introduction

Using Mac OS X Mavericks introduces you to the new version of Apple's Mac OS and is designed to help beginners and enthusiast users who want to get up and running quickly and make better use of their computers.

Mavericks is not a major update to Mac OS. There are a lot of tweaks to the interface, such as tags and tabs, new applications, such as iBooks and Maps, a new look to Pages and Keynote, and a lot more. So if you're a new Mac user, switched from Windows, or are a keen Mac user wanting to do more, I will do my best to guide you through using your Mac.

This book has been especially written in a step-by-step fashion using photography and screen prints to illustrate the steps as clearly and concisely as possible.

I hope this book is helpful to you

CHAPTER 1

Introducing Mavericks

Mac OS Mavericks is the tenth major release of Mac OS X, and at the time of writing is available from Apple free of charge. There are some new apps, such as iBooks and iMaps, plus better hardware and multiple-screen support.

The Desktop

A typical Mac desktop is shown in the following screen. The desktop is the basic working area on your Mac; it is the equivalent of your workbench or office desk.

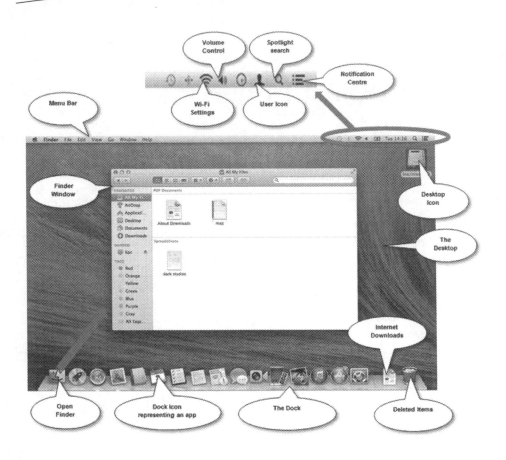

The Dock

The Dock has shortcuts to applications such as iTunes or iPhoto. If the app you are looking for isn't here, it will be in either Launchpad or the Finder (both discussed later in this chapter).

This little dot means program is open

Dock Icon representing an application

There are a couple of icons to take note of on the edge of the dock, called stacks. These are "quick access lists" that allow you to find your most recently used documents and Internet downloads.

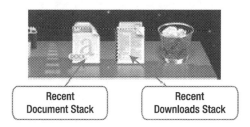

```
          Recent                    Recent
      Document Stack            Downloads Stack
```

The following screen shows what they open up as. You can see a list of recently opened documents. Also available is a list of downloads, so if you have just downloaded something from the Internet you can find it in the Downloads Stack.

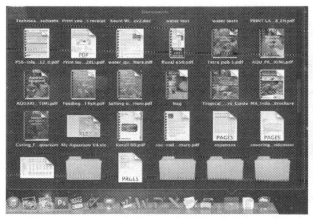 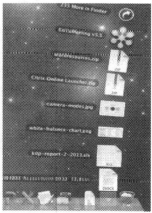

I find it useful to add my most-used icons to the dock. You can do this by dragging them to the part of the dock in which you want them to appear. I'm going to drag my Documents folder from the Finder window next to the downloads icon on the far right of the dock.

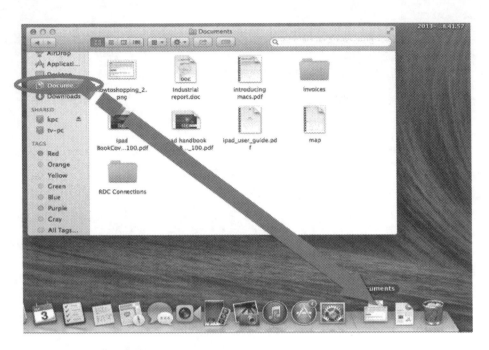

Or perhaps you want a program you use a lot to appear on the dock. A common example is Dashboard. You can drag the icon from the Apps folder in Finder. I'm going to place it in between my Launchpad icon and my Safari web browser icon. I just drag it to the dock.

Launchpad

Launchpad lets you see, organize, and easily open apps that are installed on your machine. The icons are organized into pages. To launch any application, just click on the corresponding icon.

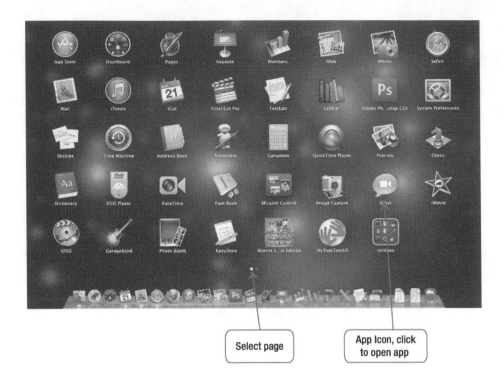

Select page

App Icon, click
to open app

To access Launchpad, click the icon on your dock.

The Menu Bar

The Menu bar consists of two main categories: Apps and Status.

App Menus

The left-hand side of the menu bar contains the menu for the app you're
currently using.

 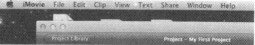

The name of the app appears in bold next to the Apple menu. There are several other app menus, often with standard names such as File, Edit, Format, Window, and Help.

Many of the commands in these menus are standard in all apps. For example, the Open command is usually in the File menu and the Copy command is usually in the Edit menu.

Status Menus

The right-hand side of the menu bar contains the status menus.

These menus give feedback on the status of your computer or give you quick access to certain features. For example, you can quickly turn on Wi-Fi, do a spotlight search, change your Mac's volume, see date and time, and check messages in Notification Center.

Finder

This is where all your documents, letters, photographs, favorite music, and so on are stored. Click the circled icon on your dock to access Finder.

Once there, you'll see that Finder is like your filing cabinet.

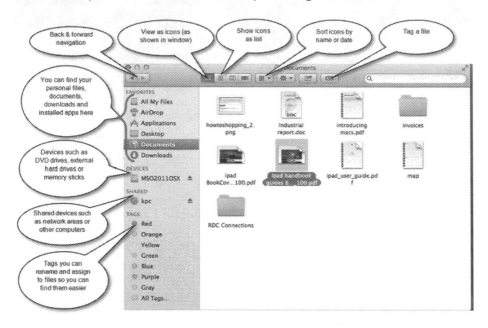

Two menus to take note of: Name and New Folder.

Name allows you to sort the icons according to their name (alphabetically) by date, or by other criteria . New Folder allows you to create new folders or perform operations on specific icons you have selected with the mouse.

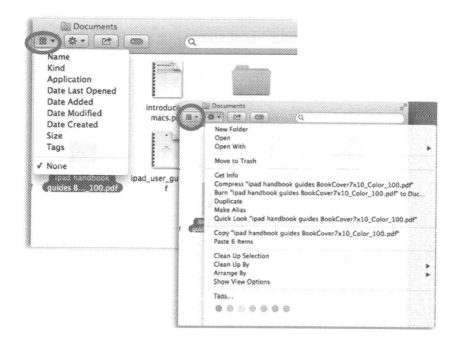

Tabs and Tags

Tabs is a new feature added to Finder that allows you to open different folders in tabs for easy access.

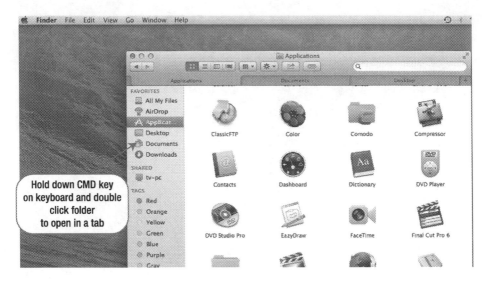

Tags allow you to place descriptive markers onto your documents to allow you to find them easier. Click the document you want to tag and select the Tags icon circled below left, and from the list select the tag that describes the category of your document, e.g., work, holiday, and so on.

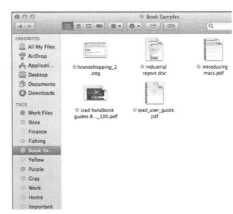

To rename the tags to something more useful, click the Finder menu, click Preferences, then click the Tags tab. As shown in the following screen, there are a variety of tags to choose from.

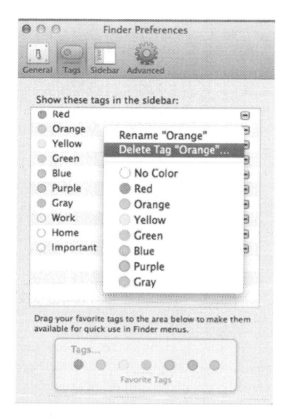

Click any of the bubbles to change the color or click the tag title to type a new name.

Highlight a tag in the sidebar and you will see all the folders that fall under that tag.

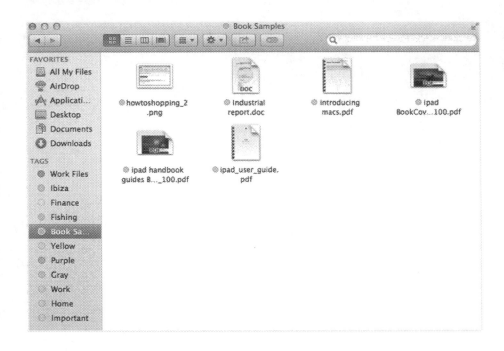

Accessing External Drives

When connected, USB flash drives and external hard disks are located in Finder under Devices.

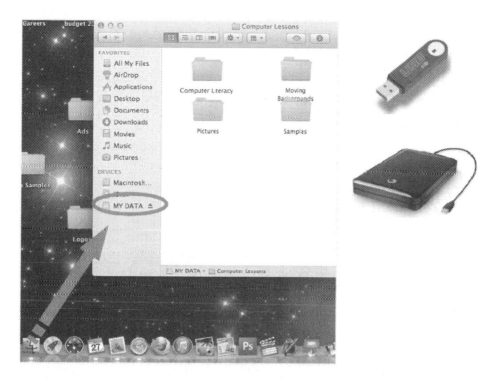

There will also be an icon representing the drive on the desktop, as shown circled here.

Note that before unplugging the device it is good practice to eject the drive by clicking on the eject icon in Finder.

Accessing CDs/DVDs

More often than not, Mac OS will automatically detect a CD or DVD you have inserted and load up the appropriate app (e.g., DVD player for DVDs, iTunes for music CDs, etc.).

If not, you can locate the disc in Finder.

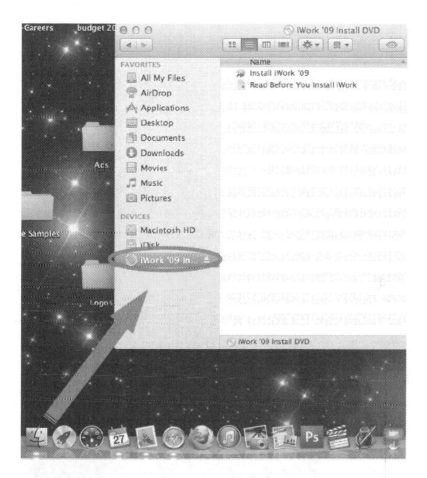

There will also be an icon on the desktop representing the CD/DVD.

To eject the CD/DVD, there is an eject button on the top right of the Mac keyboard.

Dashboard

Dashboard is a useful utility that contains "widgets"—small applications designed to accomplish a single task, such as a calculator, dictionary, clock, translator, calendar, etc. There are hundreds of widgets available; to add more click the plus sign on the bottom left-hand side of Dashboard, as shown in the following screen.

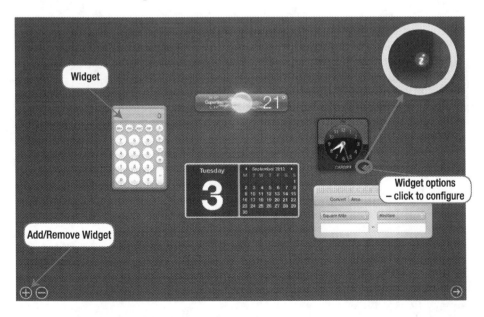

You can add widgets to your dashboard by clicking any of the icons in the following screen. You can download hundreds of different widgets for all sorts of things by clicking "More widgets...," shown at the bottom of the following screen.

Browse through and select widgets you want to install, then click on them and follow the prompts.

Notification Center

Notification Center is a tool that organizes alerts from applications. It displays those alerts until an associated action is completed. You can access Notification Center by clicking the icon on the right corner of the menu bar.

Once there, you can choose which applications you want to appear in Notification Center and how they are handled. For example, you can click a button to tweet, post status updates to Facebook, or view all notifications in the sidebar pane. Messages, such as new emails or Facebook messages, are displayed here.

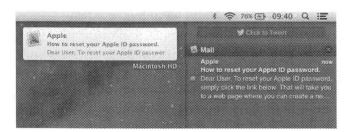

There are three types of notifications.

Banners: These are located in the upper right corner of the screen. They appear briefly and then slide off to the right. (Note that the associated application's icon is displayed on the left side of the banner, while the message from the application will be displayed on the right side.)

Alerts: These are the same as banners, but will not disappear from the screen until the user takes action.

Badges: These are red notification symbols on an application's icon that indicate the number of items available for the application.

Maps

Another great feature added to Mavericks is the Maps app. This allows you to find any location on the globe and is great for finding driving directions.

You can type the name of the city or venue you are looking for in the search field in the top right-hand corner. You can also enter postal/zip codes to find specific areas.

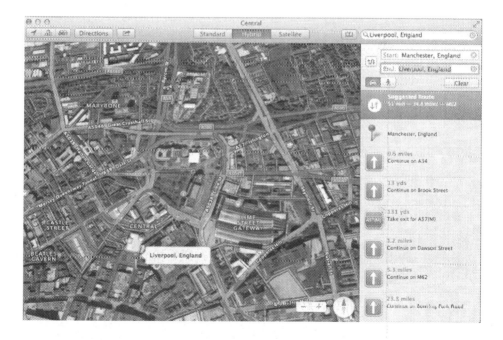

To use the directions feature all you need to do is type your location and your destination into the fields shown and Maps will come back with a route plus turn-by-turn directions for you to print or send to your iPhone.

iBooks

To open iBooks, click the iBooks icon on your Dock.

Once opened, you can search for a particular book by typing an author's name or a title into the search field on the top right of the screen.

Alternatively, you can search via the categories on the top bar. Once you have found a book you want, select it and then click Buy Book. This will download it and add it to your bookshelf in your library.

You can also click Get Sample if you want to see an excerpt before you buy. You can find all the books that you have purchased by clicking the Library button.

All your books are synchronized across all your Apple devices (iPhone, iPad and iBooks on your Mac) so you can switch between them and pick up right where you left off.

Multi-Monitor Support

Multiple displays in Mavericks work independently, so each monitor can have its own menu bar and application running at the same time. This is a big time saver.

The Dock is also available on any screen. If you are on a local network containing Apple TVs, an AirPlay icon shows up in the menu bar. You can select an Apple TV from the menu and choose to mirror your current display or to extend the desktop.

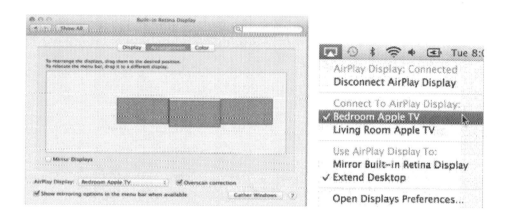

Spotlight

Spotlight is a search engine that allows you to locate anything on your Mac by typing a query. If you look in the top right-hand corner of the screen, you'll see what looks like a magnifying glass. Click that icon and type in what you're searching for.

Spotlight automatically sorts out the different types of files, such as documents, photographs, email messages, and so forth into different sections to make it easier to find.

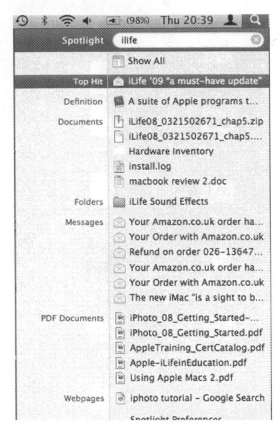

As a fun bonus, Spotlight can also give you definitions of words.

CHAPTER 2

The Cloud

You will need an Apple ID if you want to use iCloud or Apple Email or to purchase apps from the App Storeor songs from iTunes Store.

Creating an Apple ID

To create an Apple ID, open Safari and go to the following website:

appleid.apple.com

From there create an Apple ID by filling in the forms, then click Create Apple ID.

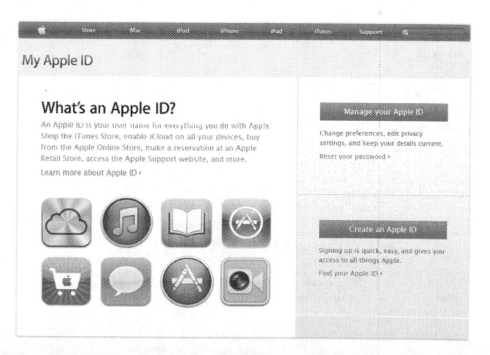

iCloud

iCloud is an online data storage service provided by Apple that allowsusers to house data (i.e., music and iOS applications) on remote servers. This data can then be downloaded to a device of your choice, such as an iPod touch, iPhone, or iPad. iCloud synchronizes email, contacts, calendars, bookmarks, notes, reminders (to-do lists), iWork documents, photos, and other data so you can access them from anywhere.

The service also allows users to back-up their iOS devices wirelessly to iCloud instead of manually doing so using iTunes. To use iCloud, on your Mac go to System Preferences from Apple Menu.

Click and open iCloud.

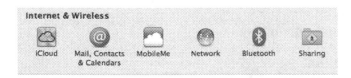

Enter your Apple ID.

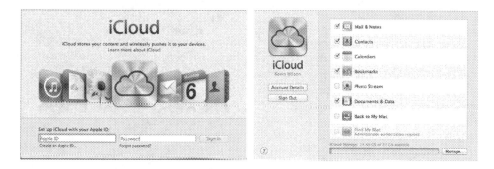

Now select which services which you want to enable on iCloud.

CHAPTER 3

App Store

The App Store is a convenient way to buy and install applications onto your Mac without the need for discs. To access the App Store, go up to your Apple Menu on the very top left of the screen and click App Store.

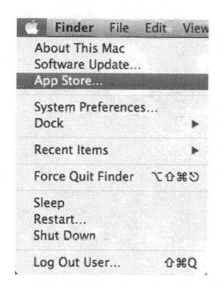

This will bring up the main store screen. You can type in the name of the app you are looking for in the top right search field or browse by category.

To buy anything, just click the price, then click Install App and sign in with your App Store/iTunes account.

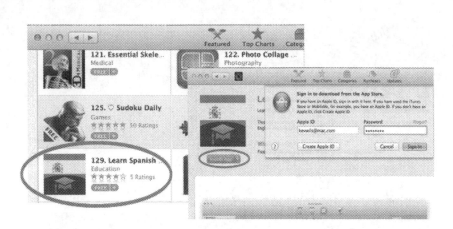

The app will now download. Once it is complete, you can find your newly installed app in Launchpad on your dock.

CHAPTER 4

Time Machine

Time Machine is a program for file backup that comes with your Mac. It works by creating incremental backups of all your files on your computer so they can be restored at a later date should you lose anything.

Time Machine also allows you to restore your whole system should your computer fail to start.

Setting Up

Connect your external hard disk to a USB port as shown here.

If you haven't yet specified a backup device for Time Machine to use, the program will ask if you would like to use the external disk for backups the first time you connect it. Click "Use as Backup Disk," and you're done.

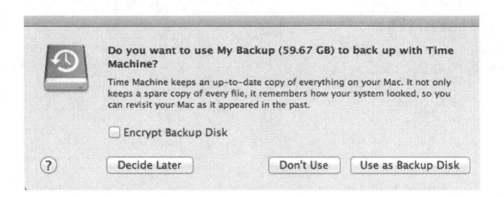

Confirmation is shown in the following screen.

Make sure you select "Show Time Machine in menu bar."

Then, whenever you want to back your files up, just connect your external hard disk and the backup will start automatically.

Restore Items

To restore something, click the icon on your menu bar as shown in the following screen. Then click "Enter Time Machine."

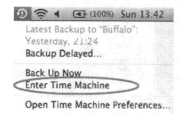

Plug in the external hard disk you used to back up your files.

Select which date to go back. All the purple highlighted dates are dates on which Time Machine made a successful backup of your files.

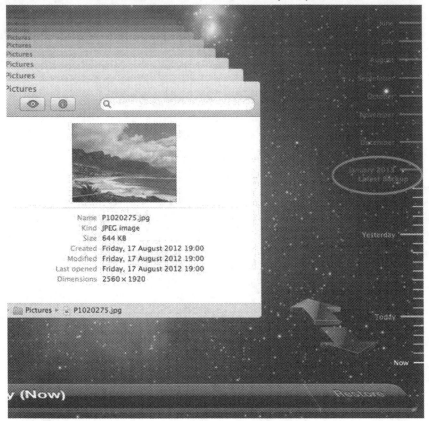

Look for the file you want to restore in the Finder window shown below by browsing through the appropriate folders in Favorites: Documents, Downloads, Movies, Music, and Pictures. Or click All My Files to view a list of all your documents.

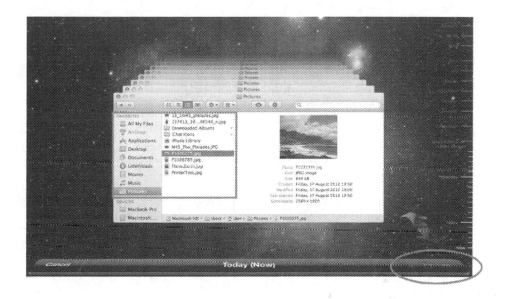

When you have found the file, click Restore on the bottom right of the screen.

CHAPTER 5

Security Considerations

I have found over the years that it is best to set up two separate accounts for yourself: Standard and Administrator. Standard is best for everyday use, such as web browsing, email, photos, music, word processing, and so on. Adminstrator is typically used only to install new software or updates—never for normal use.

The theory is that a standard user is not able to change system settings and that malicious software is less likely to do any damage because of this. Administrators have full access to all settings and all files on the system, making it a risky user account to use for normal use.

Open up the System Preferences on the Apple Menu, as shown in the following screen.

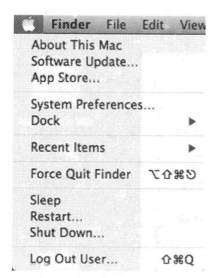

Under System, click Users & Groups, as shown in the following screen.

The left side of the following screen shows how I have my laptop set up.

User: Standard

Administrator for installing software and making system changes: kevwils

Guest User: Disabled

To add a new user click the padlock icon and enter your password. Then click the plus sign.

You can now enter your new user details.

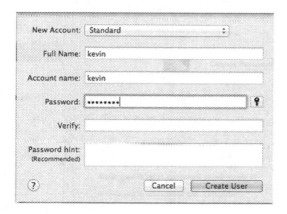

Click Create User.

Gatekeeper

Gatekeeper was introduced in Mountain Lion and OS X Lion v10.7.5 and checks for malware to help protect your Mac from misbehaving apps downloaded from the Internet. The settings are located in your System Preferences under Security & Privacy. Here you can select the appropriate options.

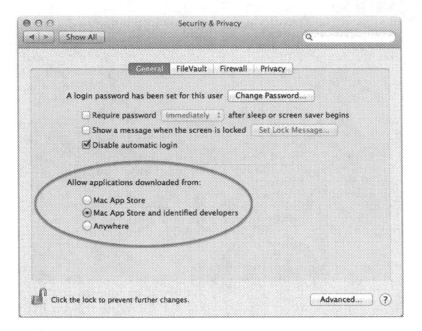

CHAPTER 6

Using the Internet

Safari is Apple's web browser.

Launching Safari

Click the Safari icon on the dock to launch the browser, as shown in the following image.

This will bring up Safari's main screen, as shown here:

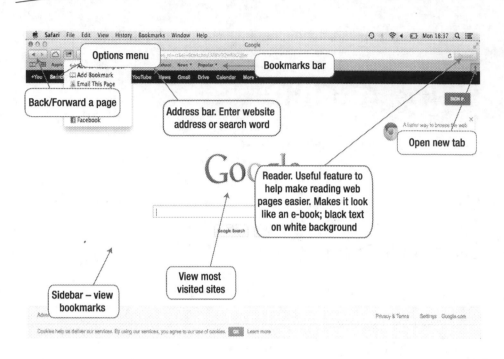

Using Safari

Start typing in the address bar. What you type doesn't have to be a website address; it can be a keyword. If, for example, we wanted to find the Amazon website, we could simply type "Amazon." The following screen shows a number of sites we can then access.

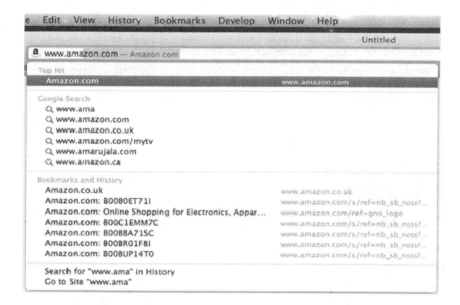

Using the Sidebar

Safari's new Sidebar houses Bookmarks, Reading List and Sharedlinks and is accessed by clicking the book-shaped icon shown here and on the top left side of the following broswer window:

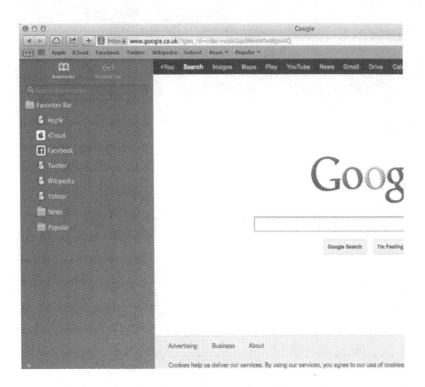

Let's quickly look at Bookmarks, one of the Sidebar's more popular features.

Bookmarking Pages

Bookmarking pages allows you to save websites without having to remember addresses or having to search for them again.

Click one of your bookmarks in the Sidebar shown in the previous screen (for example, Wikepedia). From the menu, select Add Bookmark, as shown in the next screen.

When prompted for where to save your bookmarked page ("Add this page to:" popup), choose Favorites Bar.

Your site bookmark will now appear on the Bookmarks Bar.

CHAPTER 7

Apple Email

To access your email, click the following Mail icon on the dock:

Setting Up

The first time you run the Mail program, you must set up your email account. These details are available from your service provider. Choose the type of email you have. I have an Apple ID, so I'm going to select iCloud.

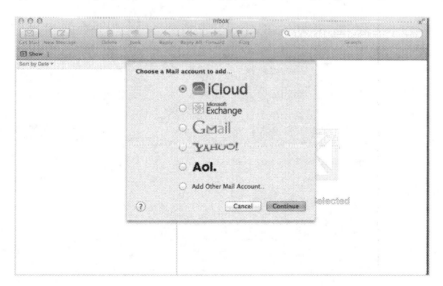

Click Continue.

Enter your Apple ID. If you don't have one, select Create Apple ID and follow the instructions. Otherwise, click Sign In.

Select what parts of your Apple ID iCloud account you want to add to Mail.

This will sync all your contacts, calendar appointments, Mail, and Safari bookmarks with your iCloud account so you can access them on any machine you sign on to.

Using Mail

Depending on your version of Mail, the main screen will look similar to this:

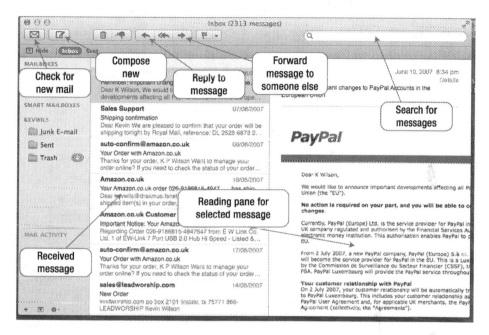

Writing a New Email

To write a new email, click the following Compose icon on the top left of the screen:

All you have to do now is fill in the fields.

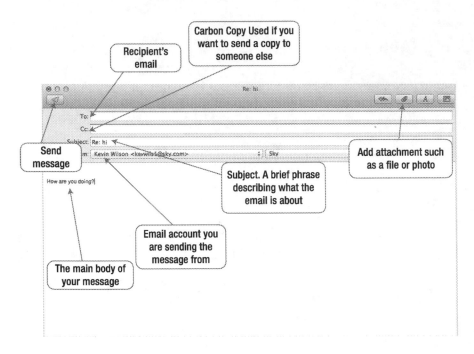

Once you are finished writing your message, click the Send Message icon on the top left.

CHAPTER 8

Calendar

iCal is useful for storing all your friends' email addresses, phone numbers, and so forth. These can be synched with your iPad, iPod touch, and/or iPhone. I find it easiest to view the calendar in Month view, as shown in the following screen:

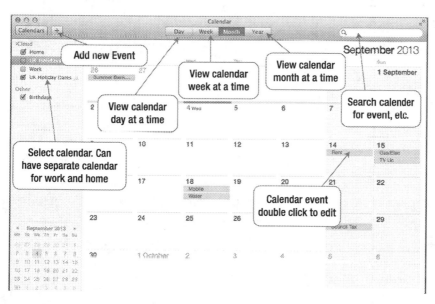

Click the following circled icon on your dock to access iCal:

Adding an Event

The quickest way to add a new event is to click on the plus sign shown in the following screen, and then enter the event name, time, and date. iCal will then add an appointment to your calendar.

A new event box will show up on the date you entered.

Here you can amend the details of the appointment. Enter a name and select the start and end times if appropriate. Also add location information and a reminder, just by filling in the necessary sections.

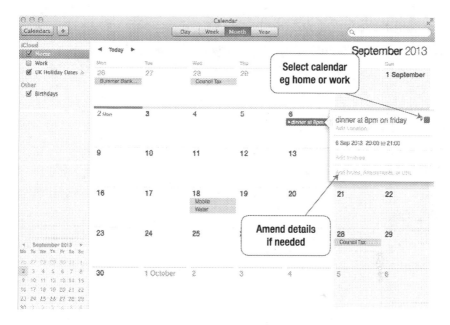

All the events will be synched with your iCloud Apple ID account, so you will be able to get your calendar on your iPhone, iPod touch, or on the Internet.

Another useful feature of iCal is that you can add calendars other people have shared and also public holidays, shift rotas, or timetables for work or college just by adding the address of the published calendar.

A common example is public holidays.

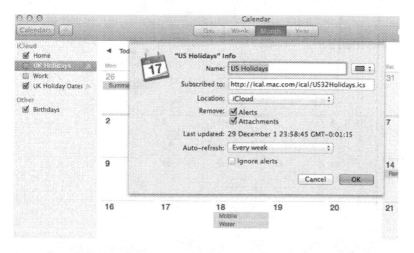

To add a public calendar, go to the File menu and select New Calendar Subscription, as shown in the following screen. Then give it an appropriate name and enter the address as shown in the "Subscribed to:" box in the previous screen.

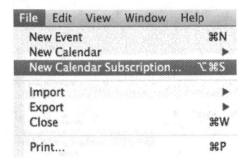

CHAPTER 9

Using iTunes

iTunes allows you to organize and manage all your music. You can purchase individual tracks or entire albums from the music store, or you can import music from an ordinary music CD. I find iTunes easier to use with the sidebar showing. To turn it on, go to your View menu within iTunes and click Show Sidebar.

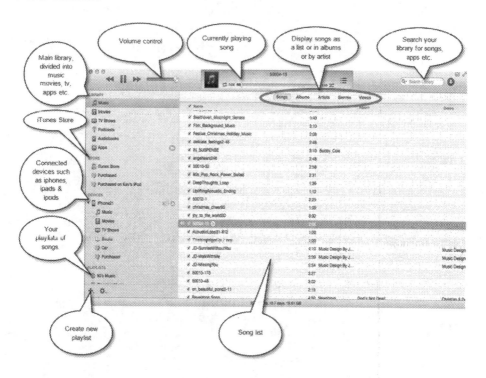

iTunes Store

From the iTunes store, click Sign In.

Enter your Apple ID and password.

If you don't have one, click Create Apple ID and follow the instructions on screen. Once you are signed in, type the song titles you want in Search Store.

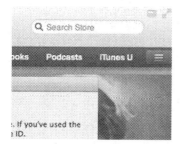

Purchase the songs. The songs will download to your Purchased playlist.

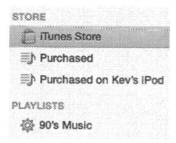

Creating Playlists

To create a new playlist, click the + sign in the bottom left-hand side of the following screen. This will add a playlist to the library. Type in the name you want to call it.

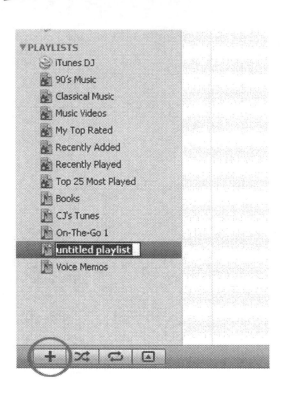

To add songs to the playlist, click Music Library, then drag the songs to your playlist as shown in the following left-hand pane. To add the playlist to your iPod device, drag the playlist from the left-hand pane of the iTunes main window to your iPod, which is listed under devices, as shown to the right.

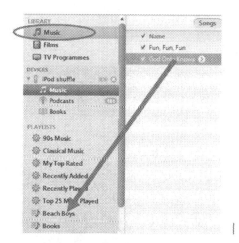
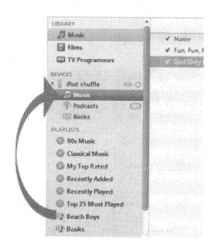

Burn a Playlist to a CD

When adding music to your CD playlist, as a guide, keep an eye on the status bar at the bottom middle of the main window; an 80-minute CD will hold 1.2 hours.

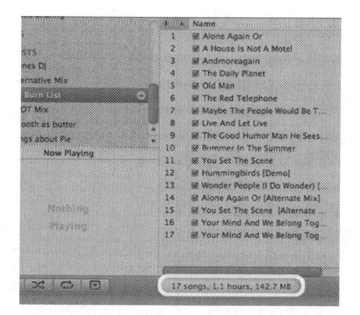

Once you have compiled your playlist, right click on it in the pane on the left-hand side. Click Burn Playlist to Disc.

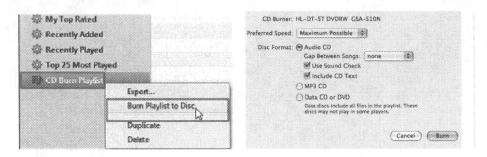

The Use Sound Check option is useful when you have made a compilation of songs from different albums. It makes sure all the songs are at the same volume level so you don't have to raise or lower the volume too much when you're listening to the CD.

Make sure the Gap Between Songs option is set to None. Insert a blank CD-R, then click Burn.

CHAPTER 10

Using iPhoto

iPhoto is a great way to store and manipulate your photographs taken from a digital camera. You can create albums and slideshows, email a photo to a friend, or post them onto Facebook. You can even put together your own album and send it to Apple. They will print you a copy and mail it to you; these are great for family albums or wedding albums. Click the iPhoto button to access the features, which are shown in the following screen.

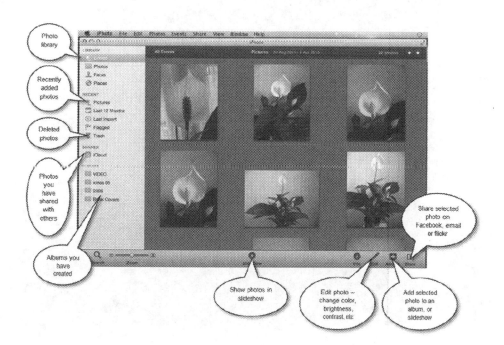

Importing Your Photos

Most digital cameras connect to your computer using a USB cable.

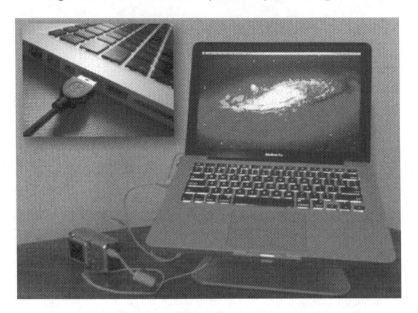

When iPhoto asks you to import the photos, enter a meaningful name for your photos. For example, the name could be "Spain Holiday," "John's Birthday 2012," etc., depending on what the photos are of. This helps you find your photos later on.

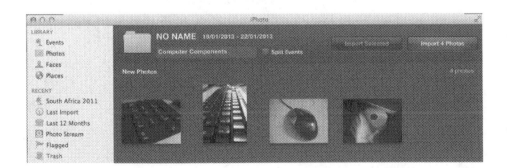

Once imported, iPhoto will ask you if you want to keep the photos on your camera or delete them.

I found it best to delete them if I have imported them into my iPhoto library. This means I have a clean camera for the next time I want to take photographs and helps eliminate duplicate photographs in the library.

Now go to your Photo library on the left-hand side, shown in the following screen.

You should now be able to see all the photos you just imported. Now this is where you can put them into albums, create slideshows, upload to Facebook, email them to friends, or create prints.

Manipulating Photos

A common problem I have come across when taking photographs with a pocket digital camera is that sometimes photos can come out a bit dark. For example, the top left photo in the following screen is very dark.

To edit the photo, double click it, then click Edit.

This brings up the following Edit screen. Click Enhance. This allows iPhoto to auto-select the best brightness and contrast settings for your photograph. It usually does a good job.

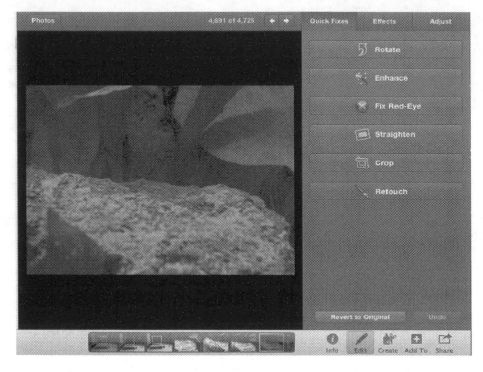

Can you see the baby fish in the photograph? Look closely.

Effects Tab

You can also experiment with different effects, such as sepia or black and white, by clicking on the Effects tab on the right-hand side.

Adjust Tab

You can also make more specific changes to your photographs using the Adjust tab. This allows you to manually change the contrast, brightness, sharpness, and so forth.

Here is a list of some of the manual adjustments you can make:

Histogram and Levels Slider: Adjust the photo's light and dark levels

Exposure: The photo's overall brightness and darkness

Contrast: The difference between light and dark areas of your photo

Saturation: Color richness. *Avoid saturating skin tones.* Keep skin tones the same while you adjust color intensity.

Definition: Improves clarity, reduces haze; affects contrast in parts of the photo

Highlights: Reduces the brightness of bright areass

Shadows: Brightens shadows to improve detail in shadowy areas

Sharpness: Crispness or softness

De-noise: Graininess, usually on dark photos

Temperature: Color tone of photo—cool has a blue tint and warm has a red tint

Tint: The photo's overall color cast

Eyedropper: Use to automatically adjust temperature and tint based on gray or white area

Editing Photos

From the Edit screen you can also rotate your photos if you took them in portrait mode on your camera, as well as crop and straighten photos.

Rotate

This rotates the image 90 degrees each time the button is clicked.

Enhance

This automatically enhances the light levels, white balance, color, and contrast of the image.

Red-eye

This feature automatically cancels out red-eye.

Straighten

This allows you to rotate an image left or right by small amounts to make the image look straight. It's useful if the camera wasn't straight when the photo was taken.

Crop

This enables you to cut the surrounding parts of an image out. When you click Crop you'll notice that a highlight window appears. This is to select the part of the image you want to keep. All the surrounding area is removed.

Retouch

This feature allows you to remove spots or blemishes on a photograph or remove an object you don't want.

Creating Albums

To create an album, click the photos you want to include (you can select multiple files by holding down the CMD key on your keyboard.

Click Add To, shown on the bottom right of the following screen.

From the menu that appears, select New Album to add to a new album. Or if you want to add the photos to an existing album, just select the album name from the menu.

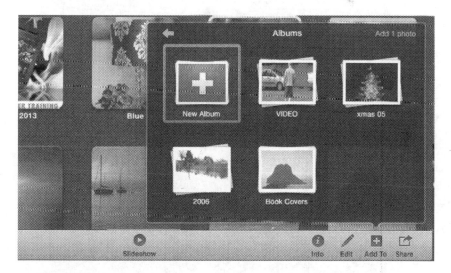

Once your album has been created it will appear in the Albums section on the left-hand side of the screen, called "untitled album." Type in a more meaningful name.

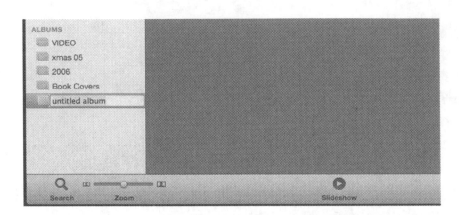

To add photographs, it's a matter of selecting photographs from the library and dragging them over to the album you just created.

Creating Slideshows

Creating a slideshow is very similar to creating an album. Select New Slideshow from the File menu. Rename the slideshow that has now appeared in the bottom left of your screen.

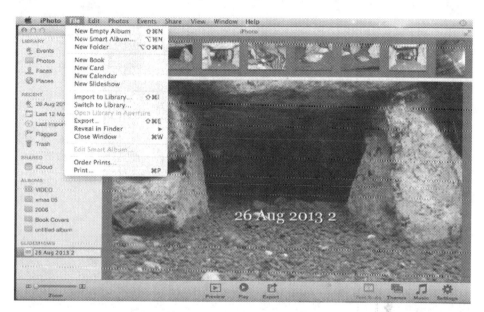

In this case, I named it Summer Holiday. Once your slideshow is created, it's just a matter of dragging in photos from your photo library as before.

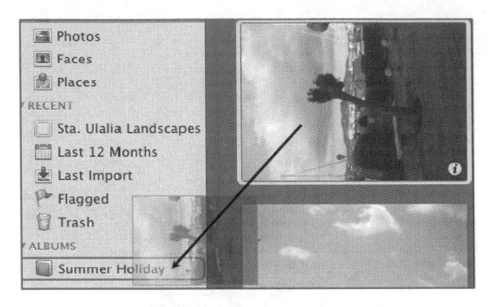

You can export your slideshow to share it with a friend by clicking Export.

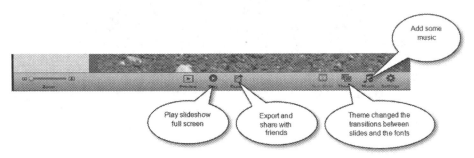

Emailing Photographs

To email a photograph to a friend, double click the appropriate image, as shown in the following screen.

Show photos
in slideshow

If this is the first time sending email through iPhoto, you will be prompted to set up an email account. The best thing is to link it to the same email account you set up in Apple mail.

My email is on iCloud, so I'm going to select that and click Setup.

Then enter full name, email address, and password. This information will have been sent to you from your service provider when you signed up.

iPhoto lets you select all sorts of fancy email templates; it's just a matter of choosing one from the list on the right-hand side.

Uploading to Facebook

Uploading photos to Facebook is simply a matter of selecting the photographs you want, as highlighted by borders in following screen. Click Share and select Facebook.

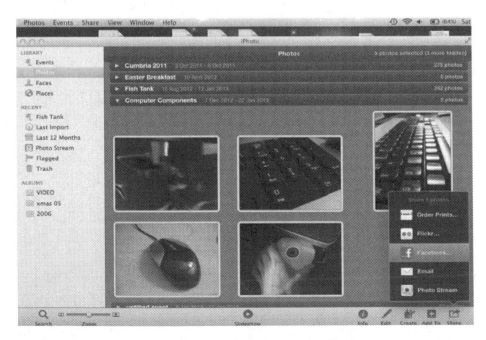

If this is your first time uploading to Facebook, iPhoto will ask for your Facebook email and password. Enter your details and click Login.

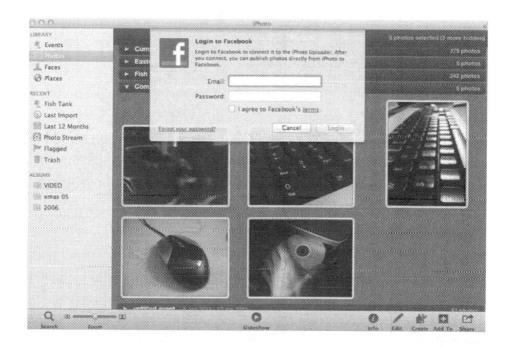

iPhoto shows you the albums currently on Facebook, under a new heading called Web on the left-hand side.

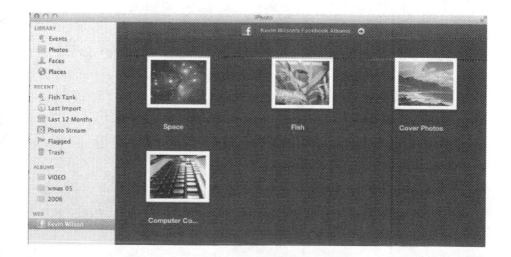

CHAPTER 11

Using iMovie

iMovie can be great for editing together your home movies. Perhaps you've just come back from your holidays, maybe a family member or friend has just gotten married, or maybe you are just collecting precious memories of your kids.

You will find iMovie on your Dock or in Finder.

Importing from Your Camera

Connect the camera to your computer with the USB cable.

Turn on your camera and set it to PC Connect mode (this mode may have a different name on your camera).

The first time you import from a device that records high-definition (HD) video, an HD Import Setting dialog appears. Even if you aren't importing high-definition video now, select Large or Full, and then click OK.

Select which video clips to import. To import all clips, set the Automatic/Manual switch to Automatic and then click Import All.

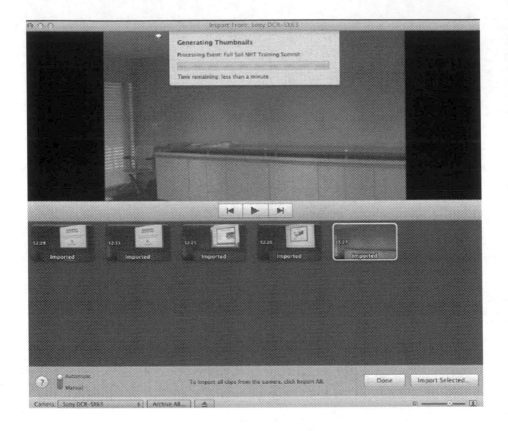

Editing Your Footage

Editing is a matter of selecting sections of your footage, as shown in the following screen, then clicking and dragging them to the project window in the top left.

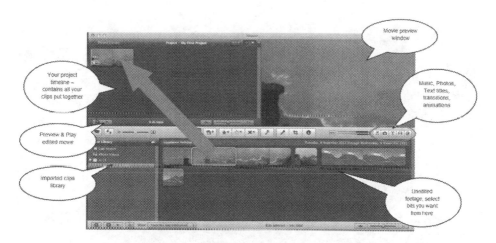

Once you are done, you will have built up a little timeline of different clips.

Transitions

You can also add transition effects between the clips in the Transitions window. To do so, click the Transitions button, circled here.

From the Transitions window, click a transition and drag it to one of the gaps between two clips on your timeline.

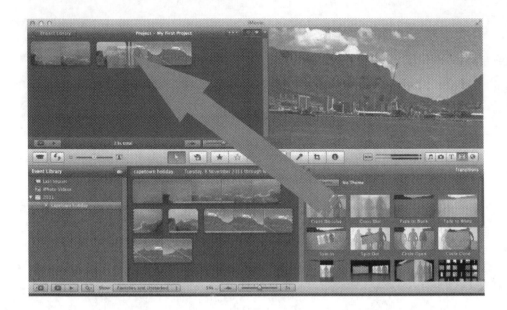

Animations

You can add little animations in the Animations window. To do so, click the Animations button, circled here.

A good one is the Map feature, which works well for vacation videos. To add one, just click and drag it onto the point on the timeline at which you want it to appear. I'm adding mine to the beginning.

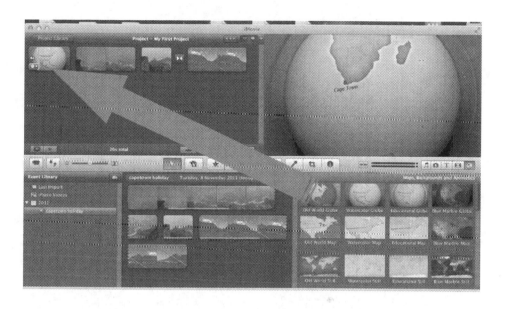

CHAPTER 12

Pages 5

Starting Pages

To launch Pages, click the Pages icon on the Dock.

Alternatively, you can find Pages on your Launchpad.

Once Pages 5 has opened, you can open a saved document or click New Document (bottom left) to open a new one.

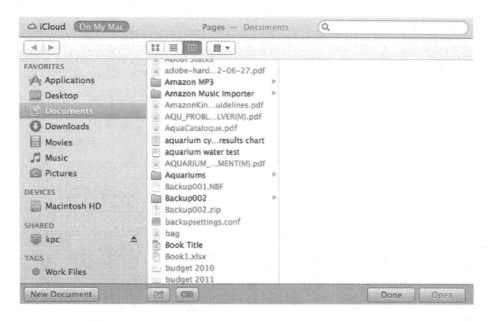

You will now need to select a template.

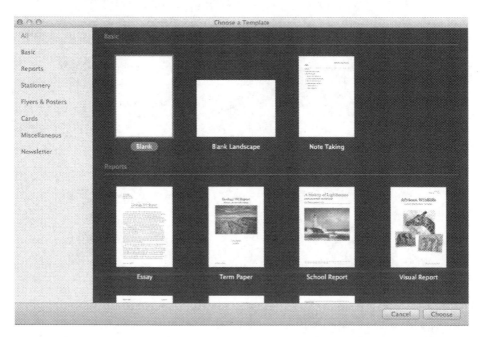

You can either select a pre-designed template or a blank one.

For this example, I am going to choose a blank template, found under the word processing section.

Once you have selected the template to use you will see the main work screen.

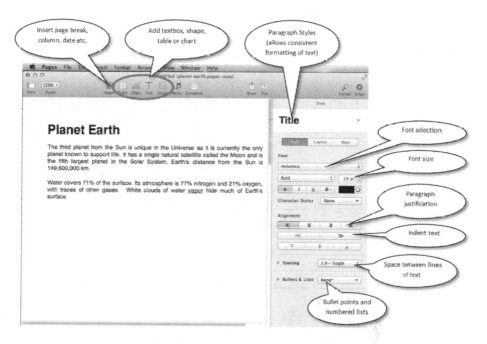

Two other sections that are hidden that are worth taking note of are Document Setup and Paragraph Styles.

Document Setup is accessed by clicking Setup, seen on the top right of the following screen. The other section is Paragraph Styles. This is a library of preset styles for headings and paragraphs that you can use.

These are marked in the following screen.

When you click on these you will see more option menus appear, as shown below.

Formatting Text

Start by creating a new document, so click New Document, as shown at the bottom right of the following screen.

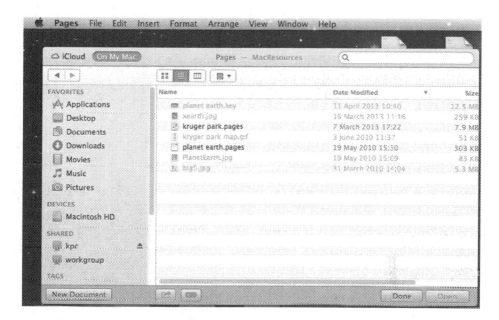

As shown in the next screen, you can either select a blank document or choose from a variety of pre-designed templates to suit your needs. For this example, select a blank template.

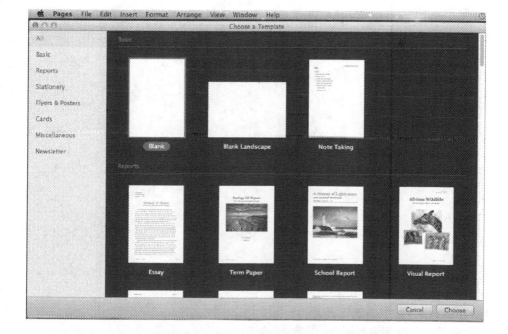

Now we need to type some text.

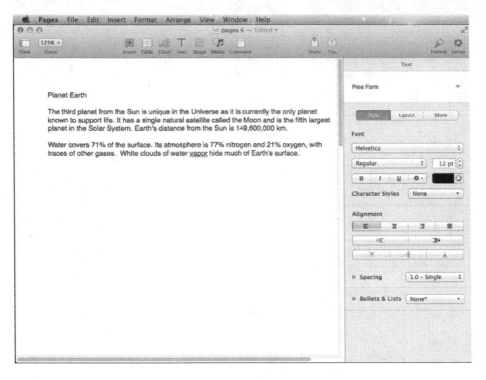

The text at the moment is very plain, so we need to format it. To format the heading, highlight it with the mouse and click Heading 1 in the paragraph styles menu.

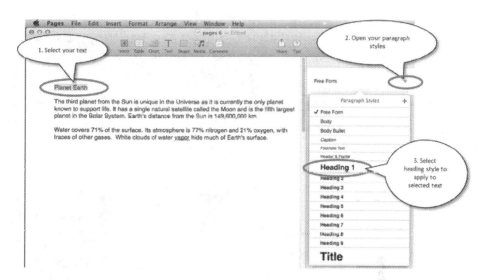

Formatting your document means laying it out in a style that is easy to read and looks attractive. This could involve changing fonts, making text bigger for headings, changing the color of text, adding graphics and photographs, and so on.

For each document template you choose from the Template Chooser, there are a number of pre-set paragraph styles. These can help you format your document consistently. For example, by ensuring all headings are the same font, size, and color.

Adding a Picture

The easiest way to add a picture is via your Finder window. Find your desired photo, then click and drag it into your document. It might be helpful to position your Finder window next to your document window, as shown in the following screen.

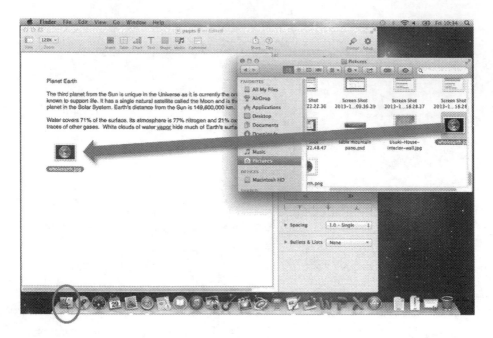

You will notice that there are sections of black around the picture you added.

To edit or format the image, click on it. You will notice that you have some new options, seen on the right-hand side.

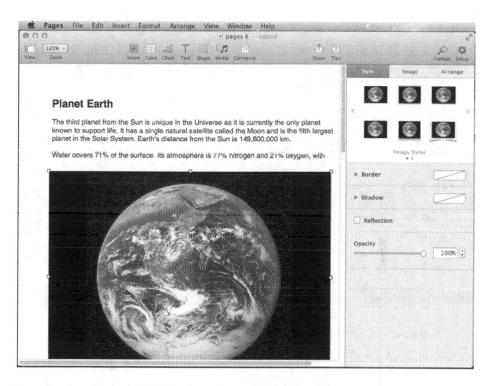

To alter the shade of the black around your image, click the Image tab on the right-hand side. Then click Instant Alpha, as shown in the following screen.

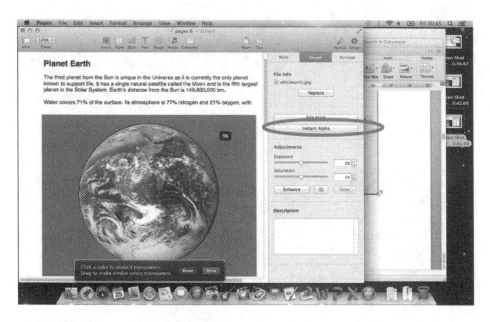

Click and hold your mouse on the black area of the image and move your mouse to the right slowly until the entire black section changes color.

Then click Done. This helps neaten up images, but it only really works when the background is significantly different from the main image. It doesn't work as well when you have crowded backgrounds in photographs, etc.

CHAPTER 13

Keynote

Keynote allows you to create multimedia presentations.

Starting Keynote

To launch Keynote, go to Launchpad and click Keynote.

Once Keynote has loaded, you can select a saved file to open. If you want to create a new presentation, click New Document, as seen on the bottom left-hand side of the following window.

From here you can choose from a variety of pre-designed templates with different themes, fonts, and colors.

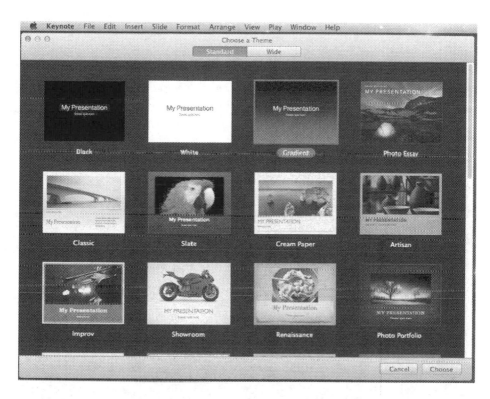

Once you have selected a template, you will see the main screen, as shown below. This is where you can start building your presentation.

Editing a Slide

Double click in the heading field, shown in the following screen, and enter a heading; for example, Planet Earth. You can click and drag the heading wherever you like.

Adding a New Slide

Click the New Slide button located on the bottom left of the screen.

Choose a slide layout from the options that appear.

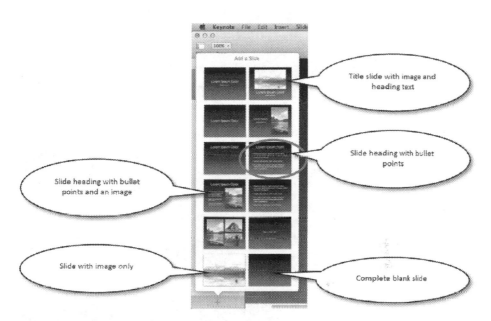

Add some text by double clicking on the text box, circled below. For example, enter the title Planet Earth.

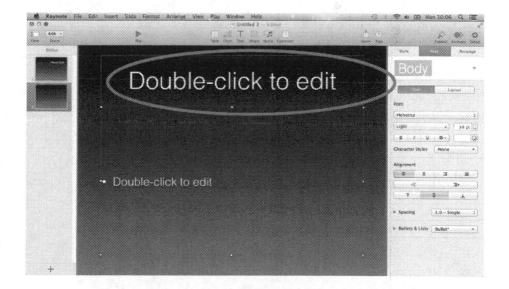

Adding Media

The easiest way to add images and media to your slides is to find them in your Finder window and then drag and drop them onto the slides.

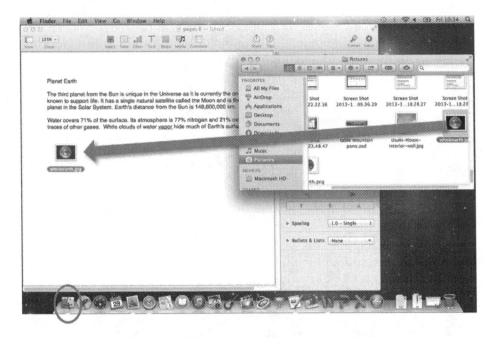

If you want photographs, they can be dragged and dropped from your iPhoto library by starting up iPhoto, finding the photograph in your library, and then dragging and dropping them onto your slide.

It helps to drag your iPhoto window over to the side, as shown above, so you can see your Keynote slide underneath.

Adding Animations

Animations allow you to make objects such as text or photographs appear.

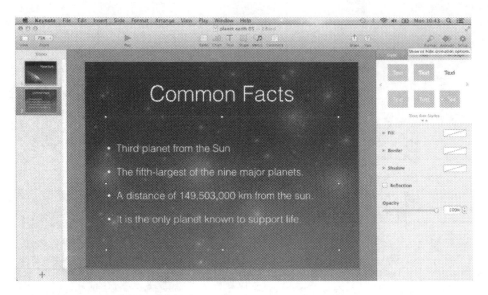

Click on your text box and select the Animate icon located on the top right corner of your screen. Then select an effect from the Effects drop-down menu (shown in the following screen).

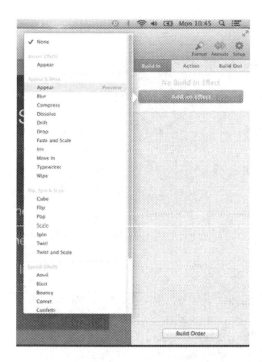 

Next, specify that you want the bullet points to appear one by one. Click the box under Delivery and select By Bullet from the drop-down menu.

To see what the effect looks like, click Preview.

Formatting Text Boxes

Click Text Box to add text, as shown below.

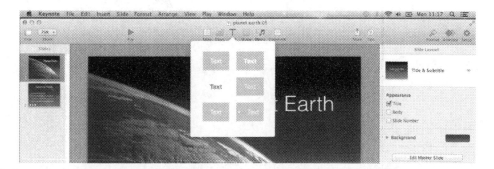

Choose a style from the drop-down menu. Enter some text into the text box.

You can format your text box by adding borders, changing fonts, changing the background color, and so forth.

To format the border and fill, click your text box and, on the right-hand side of the screen, select Style.

Formatting Text inside Text Boxes

To change the formatting of the text—for example to change the color of the text or make it bold—first select your text in the text box that you want to change. Then click the text icon on the right-hand side of your screen, as shown below.

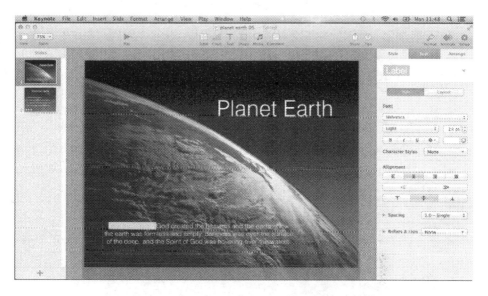

From here you can change the font, the font color, size, and so on.

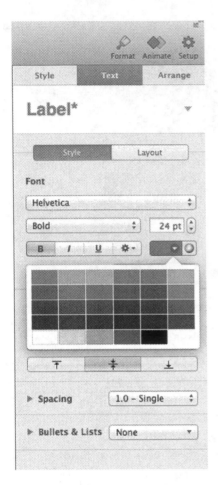

As an example, I have changed the color to dark red and made it bold. You can see what it looks like in the following screen.

Adding Styles to Text Boxes

If you wanted to change the background color (also called fill color) or add a nice border around the box, click on your text box then select the Style icon, which is located on the top right of your screen.

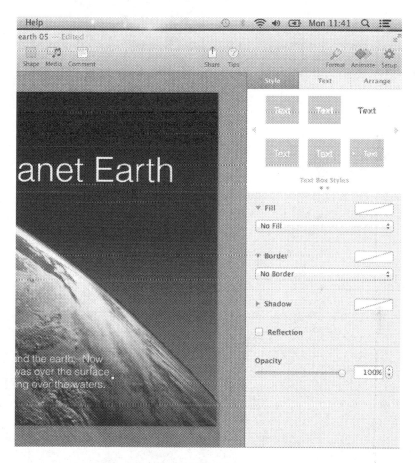

If you look down the right-hand side you will see several sections: Fill allows you to change the background color of the text box. Border allows you to add fancy borders such as picture frames and colored-line borders. Shadow allows you to add a drop-shadow effect, as if the text box is casting a shadow onto the slide.

To change the background color of the text box, click Fill, which is circled below, and select a color from the drop-down menu.

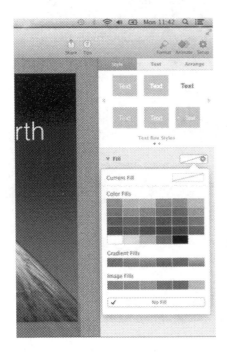
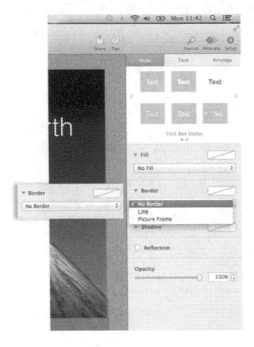

Also, if you want to add a border, under the Border section click No Border, as shown above, and change it to Picture Frame.

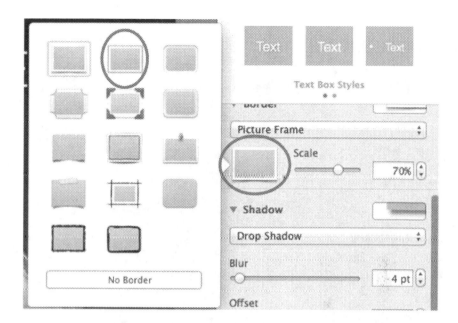

Click the "Choose frame style" button, circled above, and select a picture frame style from the menu that appears. Change the size by moving the scale slider.

Here is the result of the effect:

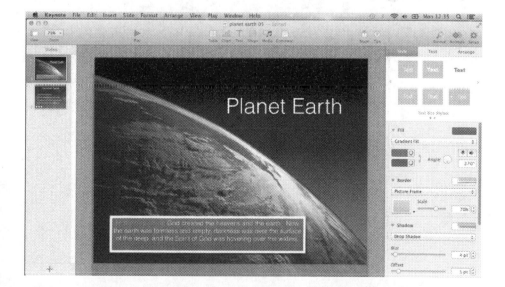

Creating a Line Chart

Select the Chart icon from the toolbar.

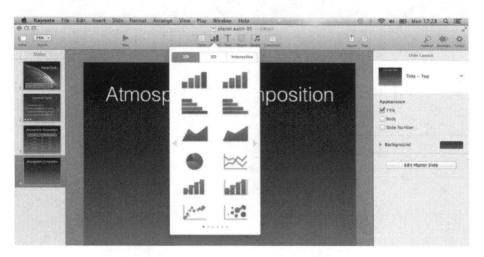

Select the Line Chart icon (fourth icon down on list). At the bottom of the chart click Edit Chart Data.

Remove the default data in the table and add your data for the chart. This example is displaying world population data over a number of years.

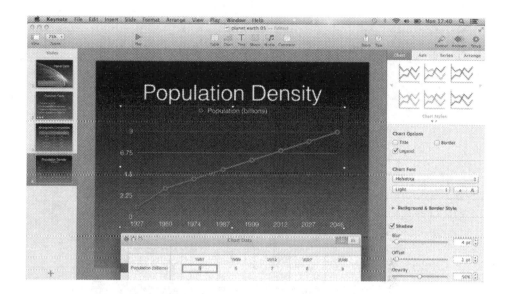

Creating Tables

To create a table click the Table icon on the toolbar. This will add a table to the current slide.

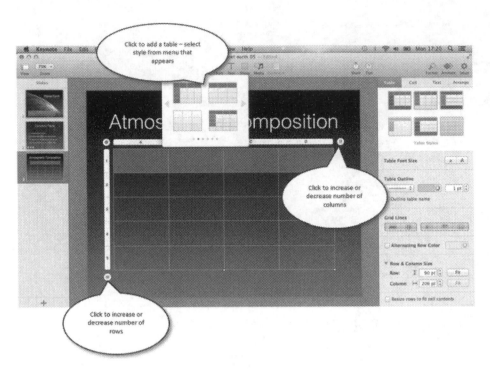

On the right-hand side of the screen, you can increase the text size, change the styles, and more. To add text to a cell in the table, double click the cell and type.

CHAPTER 14

Giving Presentations

When giving your presentations, you will likely be using a projector and a laptop. It's best to make sure both your laptop and projector are turned off before you start.

Connect to Your Computer and Projector

If the projector cable has a VGA connector, then you will need an adapter.

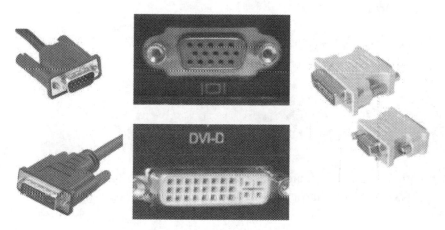

Plug the adapter into the laptop (it will only go in one way).

Then plug the other end of the adapter into the projector cable.

Plug the other end of the projector cable into the "VGA in" port on the back of the projector. The "VGA in" port is usually color-coded dark blue (on some projectors it's called "Computer in").

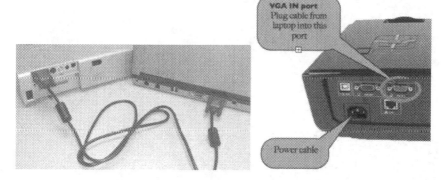

To summarize, the order will be laptop, adapter, projector cable, projector.

If you are using a ceiling-mounted projector in a classroom or boardroom, you don't usually have to worry about plugging the cable into the projector.

Plug In the projector power cord and press ON/STANDBY on the projector.

Select the Input on the Projector

Make sure the correct input is selected; for most modern projectors, this is automatic. If not, there is usually a button on the projector labeled "Input" or "Source." Press this repeatedly until the computer is displayed on the projector screen.

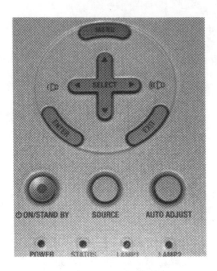

Tip: Switch on the projector first and then turn on the laptop. This allows the laptop to automatically detect the projector.

Now just launch your presentation in Keynote and you are ready to present.

If for some reason your laptop does not detect the projector, go to Finder -> Applications -> System Preferences -> Displays -> Click Display tab -> Click Detect Displays.

Select the Display

In Keynote there are two different displays: presenter and audience. The presenter version displays notes, a preview of the next slide, and so on to help you when you are giving your presentation. The other display is what your audience sees on the projector screen.

Your primary display is your laptop screen. Your secondary display is the projector screen. To make sure your audience sees the correct screen, click "Present on secondary display."

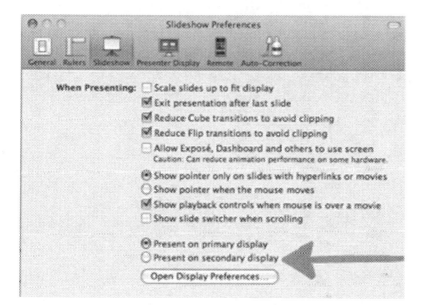

Get the eBook for only $10!

Now you can take the weightless companion with you anywhere, anytime. Your purchase of this book entitles you to 3 electronic versions for only $10.

This Apress title will prove so indispensible that you'll want to carry it with you everywhere, which is why we are offering the eBook in 3 formats for only $10 if you have already purchased the print book.

Convenient and fully searchable, the PDF version enables you to easily find and copy code—or perform examples by quickly toggling between instructions and applications. The MOBI format is ideal for your Kindle, while the ePUB can be utilized on a variety of mobile devices.

Go to www.apress.com/promo/tendollars to purchase your companion eBook.

Printed in the United States
by Baker & Taylor Publisher Services